VIKING
AFFILIATE MARKETING

Chapter 1:

Choosing an Affiliate Market Place

Overview

This course focuses on aggressively leveraging the power of YouTube to make affiliate sales. Our goal will be to establish a working affiliate apparatus and to make it profitable in as little time as possible.

If you've been looking at affiliate marketing for a while you've probably noticed that YouTube is packed with affiliate reviews of all sorts of products. Some of them are webcam talking head videos, some are selfie videos shot with a phone while taking a walk, some are impressive semi-professional videos with people behind a counter or sitting on a couch with a physical product in front of them on a coffee table, and some are basic screencast videos. And then there are even the super cheap ones that consist only of photos and text or slideshows. All of them have the same basic conclusion: "click the link below to learn more". Of course, that link is an affiliate link, and every time someone clicks it and eventually buys a product (even if it's a few days later, thanks to cookies), the person who made that video gets paid a commission. That's where we want you.

Why Video?

So why video? There's a few reasons. First: videos are more readily consumed these days than text content. People would much rather get the info they need quickly by listening and watching than by having to read. Plus, video is easier for you. Review websites and blogs simply take too much time and effort. You've got to continuously create and add textual content, proofread it, and SEO optimize all of it. And good luck getting it ranked in the search engines. In today's world, if you're not on page one (or maybe 2) of google, you're not going to get seen. For video sites like YouTube, Vimeo, and Dailymotion, on the other hand, you don't need to appear on the front page. You'll be seen in the "related videos" side bar of other similar videos. This is why it's so easy for even newbies to start seeing progress on YouTube, because everyone is constantly going from one video to the next and clicking on the related video results.

Why YouTube?

Now there are a handful of major video sites out there, but we're focusing on YouTube for the following reasons: YouTube has over a billion users – more than a third of the world's internet users! More importantly, those figures aren't remaining static. Watch time increases by 50% every year and the number of people using the site increases about 40% every year. Clearly, if you want to be seen, YouTube is the place to be!

Now that we understand why we're using video marketing, let's have a look at what we'll be learning in this course:

Chapter 1 covers affiliate networks or marketplaces. We'll be talking about how to choose and get setup with the affiliate market place that's right for you.

Chapter 2 is all about choosing a product. We'll identify ways to identify which products will perform best for you.

Chapter 3 is going to talk about the traffic method, namely the YouTube videos and how to use them effectively.

Chapter 4 is where we'll establish your battle plan and figure out how to implement what you've learned.

So, if you're ready let's dive into choosing an affiliate market place.

Why YouTube?

There are two key questions to ask before you choose an affiliate network or market place. What's your niche? Are you targeting would-be internet marketers? Survival enthusiasts? Golfers? People trying to lose weight?

The next question is whether you're trying to sell physical products or information products also called digital products. For some niches, like survival enthusiasts, you could do both. For example, an info product might be a video course or eBook on small game hunting while a physical product might be a fire starter kit or survival rations. On the other hand, some niches will primarily be one or the other. For example, the internet marketing niche will primarily just be info products while the pet reptile niche will mostly just be physical supplies. If you're in a niche where you can do both, pick the one you want to start with first and just focus on that.

If you're selling physical products, you'll be looking for online physical product stores with affiliate programs. You'll want to pick the ones with the best combination of high commission rate and popularity. For example, you might come across an online store offering a whopping 30% commission rate, but they might be lesser known and therefore you're less likely to make sales. On the other hand, a big store like Amazon, for example, might offer a low commission rate like 5-10%, but due to its popularity, you're more likely to make sales.

For info products you'll want to join one of the major digital marketplaces like ClickBank. Really all you're looking at here is ease of use and selection. Ease of use has to do with how easy it is to set up an account and start promoting products. Typically, they're all pretty easy as far as account setup, but some market places like JVZoo require you to request approval for each product and wait to be approved by the vendor while others like ClickBank allow you to pick one and start promoting immediately. Regarding selection, your number one concern is whether they have a lot of products in your niche. If you're looking for internet marketing products, JVZoo is pretty good, but ClickBank has a larger selection of both internet marketing and other niche products like weight loss, finance, carpentry, music training, and so on.

There are a ton of affiliate programs and market places out there including JVZoo, Commission Junction, LinkShare, Share-a-Sale, and the list goes on. Not to mention you can also take any eStore or product online, google their name along with the word "affiliate program" and you'll be surprised to see how many of them have their own in-house affiliate program! However, for the reasons mentioned above, this course will focus on Amazon for physical goods and ClickBank for digital ones. And that's what we'll be covering in the next lesson.

Chapter 2:

Choosing a Product

So, we're going to be looking at both ClickBank and Amazon in this lesson. We'll start by going to ClickBank.com and clicking on "Create account". Now we're not going to go through the entire account creation process as it's all pretty self-explanatory, but just note that you'll want to put an address here where you want them to send your affiliate commission checks.

Now once you've created that account you'll want to click on Affiliate Marketplace. From here, you'll be able to drill down and select the product that you want to promote. Since this is an info product marketplace we'll say we're looking for Internet Marketing products to promote. So go down to the "categories" sidebar menu and click the arrow next to "e-business" and then select "SEM & SEO" from the drop down.

In the results, you'll see hundreds of products to choose from. We'll want to pick the one that we think will be most profitable with the one caveat being this: make sure you investigate it a little afterwards to make sure it's not garbage. You want to be able to sleep with a sound conscience at night and to do that you'll want to make sure you're not promoting a rip-off. For the sake of this example, we'll assume all of these products are legit.

Now there are several ways to filter these products. For our purposes, we want to focus on three main things: Popularity, Gravity, and Earnings.

Gravity

Gravity is ClickBank's in-house measure of how well a product sells. It's based on a lot of things including number of sales and how recent those sales are. Generally anything above 30 is likely to have a solid probability of success while anything that's way up there in the hundreds might have such a high rate of sales as to indicate a ton of competition – but this isn't necessarily a bad thing.

Money

The amount of money you can expect to make per sale can be presented in terms of the initial sale commission and in the average rebill amount in the case of subscription products or products that offered something like a one-dollar trial period and then a full payment which is considered a single rebill.

You'll want to look for a balance of both of these things. But the third, popularity can be somewhat important too...

Popularity

Although gravity is usually a good measure of how well something sells, what about products that just started selling recently? Often times a hot product might launch but hasn't been around quite long enough to earn a gravity higher than 30 for example. This is where popularity might be a good thing to look at because a popular, trending product that just hit the market might not be visible if you sort just by gravity.

Let's go ahead and filter by popularity first. As you can see we've got Social Monkey at the top in popularity but it has really low gravity. This could be an indicator that it's either new or on a recent upward trend in sales but hasn't quite garnered enough sales yet to increase its gravity. Long Tail Pro, on the other hand, is in second place but has high gravity.

Now let's filter by gravity. You'll notice things are reversed here. Long Tail Pro is at the top of the charts, clearly establishing itself as a proven, successful seller. Let's have a look at the money side of things. Long Tail Pro only has an initial sale value of about a dollar or so. This is where newbies who haven't sat through our course would skip that product because of the low dollar amount. You on the other hand DID pick up our course and it's about to pay off. Pan over to the right and look at the average rebill total. Yup, over $100. If you were to click on the Long Tail Pro title, there you'd be taken to their sales page where you'd discover that they're offering a $1 10-day trial – hence the tiny initial sale value. But after those ten days are up, customers get billed at either about $40 per month or about $25 annually. Now you know where that rebill value comes from. And since those $1 trials are proven to work so darn well, the majority of customers stay the duration of the trial and then end up sticking with the product for at least one or two billing cycles. No wonder it has such a high gravity rating. There's no question that this would be a good product to promote.

To promote, simply click the promote button, enter your account nickname and copy and paste the resulting affiliate link into a notepad file. Save that for later.

Now let's move over to the amazon side of the house for physical products. Head to amazon.com and scroll all the way down to the bottom of the home page. Find the link that says "become an affiliate" and click it. This will take you to the Amazon Associates home page. Click "join for free" to set up an affiliate account. The process will be more or less the same as ClickBank. Once you've created your account, come on back to the home page. Hover over the departments button and choose a category that corresponds to your niche. For our example, we'll use camera, photo, and video. Once you're there, click the best sellers button on the top menu. This page will tell you exactly what items in this niche are selling the best updated literally every hour. This is probably one of the most valuable sales trend intelligence tools available for physical products online. Other than its best seller ranking, you'll want to just make sure the product you promote doesn't have a horrible overall feedback rating otherwise you might lose commissions due to a high refund rate.

Choose the product you want to promote and then look up at the top of your screen on the product page. After becoming an affiliate, you should have had a grey and orange bar called the amazon Associates Site Stripe at the top of your screen. When you're on a particular product page, you'll be able to use the buttons on the site stripe to immediately generate either a text link or an html short code featuring an image. Since we're focusing on YouTube for marketing and you can't put images in a YouTube description, just click on "link" and copy and paste that affiliate link into a notepad file. You'll use it later when you upload your YouTube video, which we'll cover in the next chapter.

Chapter 3:
Driving the Traffic

It's time to drive some traffic to your affiliate link. Now there are a lot of ways to do video on YouTube. If you just type any random product you can think of into the YouTube search bar along with the word review, you'll see a ton of variety. Some people are making physical product reviews in full HD with a studio-quality white background. Some are making them at their kitchen table or seated behind a counter. Some are sitting on an immaculately clean sofa in a well-lit living room with the product on a coffee table. Some of these people aren't showcasing a physical product but rather are just talking about a digital product or service. Some have lapel mics and great audio and some sound terrible. Some are real people and some are hired actors reading a script "on the cheap" from places like Fiverr or Upwork. Either way, these are all called talking head videos because they literally have the speaker on screen.

On the flip-side: you have screencast videos or slideshow style videos which are basically recordings of someone's screen or a recording of a slideshow or text and image presentation with a narration. These videos are more common for digital products but there are plenty about physical products as well. These might include software walkthroughs, pros and cons lists, product comparisons, or even people just restating the advertised features of the product.

Regardless of which style you choose to use; the good news is you don't need to worry about making these studio quality.

Most people who search for "such-and-such product review" are simply looking for information and assurance that they aren't wasting money. They could care less if you have Hollywood-level audio, professional lighting, or even a clean house behind you. In fact, if a video looks too professional, they might suspect that it's not completely natural or honest. Ironically, this is where looking and sounding a bit less classy and more down-to-earth actually works in your favor. People tend to trust people who they think are just ordinary fellow consumers more than fancy presenters who seem to have a lot of money behind their production.

So how do you make these videos? Well that's easy! If you're making a "talking head" video, you'll just need a smartphone or a webcam. That's literally it. If you're doing a slideshow style video, you can use something like windows movie maker (just insert text and images) or you can even export a PowerPoint presentation to .mp4 video. For screencast/screen recording videos, use a screen capture software like Snagit or Screencast-o-matic.

Once you've uploaded your video file to YouTube (just sign in to your account and find the upload button) you'll want to start optimizing it. Be sure to use at least the name of the product and the word "review" in your video title. You can also type in the year, to show it's a newer review. Another thing you might consider is adding the word discount to help your chances of being seen if people are looking for a lower price on the product. Just make sure it's true. For example: if you're promoting or reviewing a product on Amazon and, like many of their products, the price is significantly marked down from retail, then it's perfectly okay to use the word discount in your title.

As for your description: you want to make this as wordy and keyword rich as you can. Right at the top you'll want your Call-to-Action or CTA and your affiliate link. This could be something like "click here to learn more" or "use this link to get it now". Or you could get a little more creative and use the discount percentage in your CTA. For example, let's say you're looking at a wallet on Amazon and it's on sale for about $22 but has a retail price of around $75. In that case, it would be perfectly fair and legitimate to say "save 70% when you buy through this link". And then, of course, paste your link in there. But that's just the first couple lines you want your viewers to see. You'll want to pack even more in there. If you have a script that you used for the video, just paste that in there. If not, just summarize what you wrote. Keep in mind you want to ensure your main keywords, namely the product name and the word review, appear in your description at least a few times for SEO purposes. But don't make it so spammy that it gets flagged.

Finally, you'll want to choose good keyword tags. Try to find as many ways of saying your product's name and the word review as possible. For example: "X review" and "review of X" are two completely different tags that will contribute different SEO values.

That's about all there is to uploading your video. You can now sit back and let YouTube's search algorithms do the work for you or you can start doing some social sharing and posting. Post a link to the video on Facebook and Twitter. If you have a blog, embed the video in a post there. These backlinks will have the dual purpose of driving real traffic as well as slightly boosting your SEO.

Oh, and one last tip: it's been reported that literally asking, both in the video and in the description, for people to "like, comment, subscribe" can genuinely increase your likes, comments, and subscriptions. Consider using such a CTA in your video too. Maybe get creative and invite people to opine or disagree with your assessment in the comments section. The more engagement the better.

That's it for this lesson. If you're ready, let's move into the final lesson: establishing your battle plan.

Chapter 4:
Battle Plan

The number one reason most people never succeed in online marketing is inaction. So, before we even begin with step one of our battle plan you need to make a resolution to start taking action right now. Everything you learned in this course can be applied and executed right now in as little as an hour (although if it's your first time it may take longer). And there's one more resolution you need to make: a willingness to take imperfect action. The prime driver for inaction is the never-ending vision of the "perfect execution". Set that aside. Don't throw it away, there'll be time for it later. Just set it aside for now and start taking IMPERFECT action. Knock out the steps below, even if you're not sure about what niche you'll ultimately end up in.

Let's get started:

Battle Plan

Step 1: Determine your niche. If you aren't sure what your ideal niche is, just pick one and go with it – you can rinse and repeat with another niche later.

Step 2: Choose which affiliate marketplace/network you'll be using and create your account.

Step 3: Select a product and copy your affiliate link.

Step 4: Figure out how you're going to do your video (talking head, screencast, etc.) and start recording.

Step 5: Upload your video and optimize your title, description, and tags.

Step 6: Choose another product and start steps 3 through 5 over again.

Don't get discouraged if you don't get many views or sales or if there was more competition for the product than you expected. Instant success is not only uncommon, it's also not what we're aiming for. Once you have done this process a few times you'll be super-fast at it and you'll be able to do more and more product promotions in less and less time. All of those videos WILL pay off in time.

So there you have it. There's your battle plan for getting started with affiliate marketing. Stop procrastinating and start earning commissions TODAY!